THE SIMPLE WISDOM OF
POPE FRANCIS

THE JOY OF EVANGELIZATION

Libreria Editrice Vaticana

United States Conference of Catholic Bishops
Washington, DC

Cover image: CNS photo/Paul Haring

First printing, November 2013

ISBN: 978-1-60137-452-3

CONTENTS

INTRODUCTION

You have in your possession one of the volumes of *The Simple Wisdom of Pope Francis* series, the first compilation of Pope Francis's teachings.

Immediately after his election on March 13th 2013, the world turned their eyes to the new Successor of Peter to notice Pope Francis's simple ways, humbleness, and his love for the poor and the sick.

This collection captures the wisdom of Pope Francis during his general audiences, which are regularly held on Wednesdays when the pope is in Rome. The general audiences give pilgrims and visitors a chance to "see the pope" and receive the Papal Blessing, or Apostolic Blessing, from the successor of the Apostle Peter. General audiences with the pope are spoken mainly in Italian but also in English, French, Spanish or other languages depending on the groups visiting. They consist of short, scripturally-based teachings in which the pope instructs the faithful across the world.

A final note: Francis's teachings also embrace the Year of Faith, which was instituted by our previous pope, Benedict XVI. The Year of Faith was "a summons to an authentic and renewed conversion to the Lord, the one Savior of the world" and spanned from October 11, 2012, through November 24, 2013. Pope Francis also references the *Catechism of the Catholic Church*, which is an organized presentation of the essential teachings of the Catholic Church.

It is our prayer that the teachings of the Holy Father within this series will be a source of hope and help in embracing the grace of faith a little more each day.

WE FEEL THE JOY OF EVANGELIZING

MAY 22, 2013

ST. PETER'S SQUARE

Dear Brothers and Sisters, good morning!

In the Creed, immediately after professing our faith in the Holy Spirit, we say: "I believe in one, holy, catholic and apostolic Church." There is a profound connection between these two realities of faith: indeed it is the Holy Spirit who gives life to the Church, who guides her steps. Without the constant presence and action of the Holy Spirit the Church could not live and could not carry out the task that the Risen Jesus entrusted to her: to go and make disciples of all nations (cf. Mt 28:19).

Evangelizing is the Church's mission. It is not the mission of only a few, but it is mine, yours and our mission. The Apostle Paul exclaimed: "Woe to me if I do not preach the Gospel!" (1 Cor 9:16). We must all be evangelizers, especially with our life! Paul VI stressed that "evangelizing is . . . the grace and vocation proper to the Church, her deepest identity. She exists in order to evangelize" (Apostolic Exhortation *Evangelii Nuntiandi*, no. 14).

Who is the real driving force of evangelization in our life and in the Church? Paul VI wrote clearly: "It is the Holy Spirit who today, just as at the beginning of the Church, acts in every evangelizer who allows himself to be possessed and led by him. The Holy Spirit places on his lips the words which he could not find by himself, and at the same time the Holy Spirit predisposes the soul of the hearer to be open and receptive to the Good News and to the Kingdom being proclaimed" (*ibid.*, no. 75). To evangelize, therefore, it is necessary to open ourselves once again to the horizon of God's Spirit, without being afraid of what he asks us or of where he leads us. Let us entrust ourselves to him! He will enable us to live out and bear witness to our faith, and will illuminate the heart of those we meet.

This was the experience at Pentecost. "There appeared" to the Apostles gathered in the Upper Room with Mary, "tongues as of fire, distributed and resting on each one of them. And they were all filled with the Holy Spirit and began to speak in other tongues, as the Spirit gave them utterance" (Acts 2:3-4). In coming down upon the Apostles the Holy Spirit makes them leave the room they had locked themselves into out of fear, he prompts them to step out of themselves and transforms them into heralds and witnesses of the "mighty works of God" (v. 11). Moreover this transformation brought about by the Holy Spirit reverberated in the multitude that had arrived "from every nation under heaven" (v. 5) for each one heard the Apostles' words as if they had been "speaking in his own language" (v. 6).

This is one of the first important effects of the action of the Holy Spirit who guides and brings to

> **To evangelize it is necessary to open ourselves to the horizon of God's Spirit, without being afraid of where he leads us.**

life the proclamation of the Gospel: unity, communion. It was in Babel, according to the Biblical account, that the dispersion of people and the confusion of languages had begun, the results of the act of pride and conceit of man who wanted to build with his efforts alone, without God, "a city, and a tower with its top in the heavens" (Gn 11:4). At Pentecost these divisions were overcome. There was no longer conceit with regard to God, nor the closure of some people to others; instead, there was openness to God, there was going out to proclaim his word: a new language, that of love which the Holy Spirit pours out into our hearts (cf. Rom 5:5); a language that all can understand and that, once received, can be expressed in every life and every culture. The language of the Spirit, the language of the Gospel, is the language of communion which invites us to get the better of closedness and indifference, division and antagonization.

> **What do I do with my life? Do I create unity around me? Or do I cause division, by gossip, criticism or envy? What do I do?**

We must all ask ourselves: How do I let myself be guided by the Holy Spirit in such a way that my life and my witness of faith is both unity and communion? Do I convey the word of reconciliation and of love, which is the Gospel, to the milieus in which I live. At times it seems that we are repeating today what happened at Babel: division, the incapacity to understand one another, rivalry, envy, egoism. What do I do with my life? Do I create unity around me? Or do I cause division, by gossip, criticism or envy? What do I do? Let us think about this.

Spreading the Gospel means that we are the first to proclaim and live the reconciliation, forgiveness, peace, unity and love which the Holy Spirit gives us. Let us remember Jesus' words: "By this all men will know that you are my disciples, if you have love for one another" (Jn 13:34-35).

A second element is the day of Pentecost. Peter, filled with the Holy Spirit and standing "with the eleven," "lifted up his voice" (Acts 2:14) and "confidently" (v. 29), proclaimed the Good News of Jesus, who gave his life for our salvation and who God raised from the dead. This is another effect of the Holy Spirit's action: the courage to proclaim the newness of the Gospel of Jesus to all, confidently (with parrhesia), in a loud voice, in every time and in every place.

Today too this happens for the Church and for each one of us: the fire of Pentecost, from the action of the Holy Spirit, releases an ever new energy for mission, new ways in which to proclaim the message of salvation, new courage for evangelizing. Let us never close ourselves to this action! Let us live the Gospel humbly and courageously!

Let us witness to the newness, hope and joy that the Lord brings to life. Let us feel within us "the delightful and comforting joy of evangelizing" (Paul VI, Apostolic Exhortation, *Evangelii Nuntiandi*, no. 80). Because evangelizing, proclaiming Jesus, gives us joy. Instead, egoism makes us bitter, sad, and depresses us. Evangelizing uplifts us.

I will only mention a third element, which, however, is particularly important: a new evangelization, a Church which evangelizes, must always start with prayer, with asking, like the Apostles in the Upper Room, for the fire of the Holy Spirit. Only a faithful and intense relationship with God makes it possible to get out of our own closedness and proclaim the Gospel with parrhesia. Without prayer our acts are empty, and our proclamation has no soul, it is not inspired by the Spirit.

Dear friends, as Benedict XVI said, today the Church "feels the wind of the Holy Spirit who helps us, who shows us the right road; and so, we are on our way, it seems to me, with new enthusiasm, and we thank the Lord" (*Address to the Ordinary Assembly of the Synod of Bishops*, October 27, 2012). Let us renew every day our trust in the Holy Spirit's action, the trust that he acts within us, that he is within us, that he gives us apostolic zeal, peace and joy. Let us allow him to lead us. May we be men and women of prayer who witness to the Gospel with courage, becoming in our world instruments of unity and of communion with God. Thank you.

Friday, May 24, is the day dedicated to the liturgical Memorial of the Blessed Virgin Mary, Help of Christians, venerated with deep devotion at the Shrine of Sheshan in Shanghai.

I ask all the world's Catholics to join in prayer with the brothers and sisters who are in China, to implore from God the grace to proclaim humbly and joyfully Christ who died and was raised, to be faithful to his Church and to the Successor of Peter, and to live daily life in the service of their country and their fellow citizens, in a manner consistent with the faith they profess.

Making our own a few words of the prayer to Our Lady of Sheshan, I would like to invoke Mary with you in this way: "Our Lady of Sheshan, support the commitment of all those in China who among their daily labors continue to believe, to hope and to love, so that they may never be afraid to talk to the world about Jesus and about the world to Jesus."

Mary, faithful Virgin, sustain Chinese Catholics, make their challenging tasks ever more precious in the eyes of the Lord, and give growth to the affection and participation of the Church which is in China on the journey of the universal Church.

THE TRINITY, THE FACE WITH WHICH GOD REVEALED HIMSELF

SOLEMNITY OF THE MOST HOLY TRINITY

MAY 26, 2013

ST. PETER'S SQUARE

Dear Brothers and Sisters,

Good morning! This morning I made my first visit to a parish in the Diocese of Rome. I thank the Lord and I ask you to pray for my pastoral service to this Church of Rome whose mission is to preside in universal charity.

Today is the Sunday of the Most Holy Trinity. The light of Eastertide and of Pentecost renews in us every year the joy and amazement of faith: let us recognize that God is not something vague, our God is not a God "spray," he is tangible; he is not abstract but has a name: "God is love." His is not a sentimental, emotional kind of love but the love of the Father who is the origin of all life, the love of the Son who dies on the Cross and is raised, the love of the Spirit who renews human beings and the world. Thinking that God is love does us

> **Our God is not a God "spray," he is tangible; he is not abstract but has a name: "God is love."**

so much good, because it teaches us to love, to give ourselves to others as Jesus gave himself to us and walks with us. Jesus walks beside us on the road through life.

The Most Holy Trinity is not the product of human reasoning but the face with which God actually revealed himself, not from the heights of a throne, but walking with humanity. It is Jesus himself who revealed the Father to us and who promised us the Holy Spirit. God walked with his people in the history of the People of Israel and Jesus has always walked with us and promised us the Holy Spirit who is fire, who teaches us everything we do not know and from within us guides us, gives us good ideas and good inspirations.

Today we do not praise God for a specific mystery, but for himself, "for his immense glory," as the liturgical hymn says. We praise him and we thank him because he is Love, and because he calls us to enter into the embrace of his communion which is eternal life.

Let us entrust our praise to the hands of the Virgin Mary. She, the most humble of creatures, thanks to Christ has already arrived at the destination of the earthly pilgrimage: she is already in the glory of the Trinity. For this reason Mary our Mother, Our Lady, shines out for us as a sign of sure hope. She is the Mother of Hope; on our journey, on our way, she is Mother of Hope. She is also the Mother who comforts us, the Mother of consolation and the Mother who accompanies us on the journey. Let us now pray to Our Lady all together, to Our Mother who accompanies us on the way.

Dear Brothers and Sisters,

Fr. Giuseppe Puglisi, a priest and martyr, killed by the Mafia in 1993, was beatified yesterday in Palermo. Fr. Puglisi was an exemplary priest, especially dedicated to the pastoral care of youth. In teaching boys in accordance with the Gospel he saved them from the criminal underworld and thus the latter sought to get the better of him by killing him. However, in fact it is he who won, with the Risen Christ. I think of all the suffering of men and women, and also of children, who are exploited by so many forms of mafia, which exploit them by forcing them to do a job that enslaves them, with prostitution, with so many social pressures. Behind this exploitation, behind this slavery, there are "mafias." Let us pray the Lord to convert the heart of these people. They cannot do this! They cannot make slaves of us, brothers and sisters! We must pray to the Lord! Let us pray that these members of the mafia be converted to God and let us praise God for the luminous witness borne by Fr. Giuseppe Puglisi, and let us set store by his example!

Have a good Sunday and a good lunch!

THE CHURCH, THE FAMILY OF GOD'S CHILDREN

MAY 29, 2013

ST. PETER'S SQUARE

Dear Brothers and Sisters, good morning!

Last Wednesday I emphasized the deep bond between the Holy Spirit and the Church. Today I would like to begin some catecheses on the mystery of the Church, a mystery which we all experience and of which we are part. I would like to do so with some concepts that are evident in the texts of the Second Vatican Ecumenical Council.

Today the first one is: "The Church as the family of God."

In recent months I have more than once mentioned the Parable of the Prodigal Son or, rather, of the Merciful

Father (cf. Lk 15:11-32). The younger son leaves his father's house, squanders all he has and decides to go home again because he realizes he has erred. He no longer considers himself worthy to be a son but thinks he has a chance of being hired as a servant. His father, on the contrary, runs to meet him, embraces him, restores to him his dignity as a son and celebrates. This parable, like others in the Gospel, clearly shows God's design for humanity.

What is God's plan? It is to make of us all a single family of his children, in which each person feels that God is close and feels loved by him, as in the Gospel parable, feels the warmth of being God's family. The Church is rooted in this great plan. She is not an organization established by an agreement

> **What is God's plan? It is to make of us all a single family of his children, in which each person feels that God is close and feels loved by him.**

between a few people, but—as Pope Benedict XVI has so often reminded us—she is a work of God, born precisely from this loving design which is gradually brought about in history. The Church is born from God's wish to call all people to communion with him, to friendship with him, indeed, to share in his own divine life as his sons and daughters. The very word "Church," from the

Greek *ekklesia*, means "convocation": God convokes us, he impels us to come out of our individualism, from our tendency to close ourselves into ourselves, and he calls us to belong to his family.

Furthermore this call originates in creation itself. God created us so that we might live in a profound relationship of friendship with him, and even when sin broke off this relationship with him, with others and with creation, God did not abandon us. The entire history of salvation is the story of God who seeks out human beings, offers them his love and welcomes them. He called Abraham to be the father of a multitude, he chose the People of Israel to make a covenant that would embrace all peoples, and in the fullness of time, he sent forth his Son so that his plan of love and salvation might be fulfilled in a new and eternal Covenant with the whole of humanity.

When we read the Gospels, we see that Jesus gathers round him a small community which receives his word, follows it, shares in his journey, becomes his family, and it is with this community that he prepares and builds his Church.

So what is the Church born from? She is born from the supreme act of love of the Cross, from the pierced side of Jesus from which flowed blood and water, a symbol of the sacrament of the Eucharist and of Baptism. The lifeblood of God's family, of the Church, is God's love which is actualized in loving him and others, all others, without distinction or reservation. The Church is a family in which we love and are loved.

When did the Church manifest herself? We celebrated it two Sundays ago; she became manifest when the gift of the Holy Spirit filled the heart of the Apostles and spurred them to go out and begin their journey to proclaim the Gospel, spreading God's love.

Still today some say: "Christ yes, the Church no." Like those who say "I believe in God but not in priests." But it is the Church herself which brings Christ to us and which brings us to God. The Church is the great family of God's children. Of course, she also has human aspects. In those who make up the Church, pastors and faithful, there are shortcomings, imperfections and sins. The Pope has these too—and many of them; but what is beautiful is that when we realize we are sinners we encounter the mercy of God who always forgives. Never forget it: God always pardons and receives us into his love of forgiveness and mercy. Some people say that sin is an offense to God, but also an opportunity to humble oneself so as to realize that there is something else more beautiful: God's mercy. Let us think about this.

> **When we realize we are sinners we encounter the mercy of God who always forgives.**

Let us ask ourselves today: How much do I love the Church? Do I pray for her? Do I feel part of the family of the Church? What do I do to ensure that she is a community in which each one feels welcome and understood, feels the mercy and love of God who renews life? Faith is a gift and an act which concern us personally, but God calls us to live with our faith together, as a family, as Church.

Let us ask the Lord, in a very special way during this Year of Faith, that our communities, the whole Church, be increasingly true families that live and bring the warmth of God.

⁂

I cordially greet those from Poland who came to this audience. I now turn my thoughts to the young people who will meet on June 1 in the fields of Lednica. Dear young friends! I join with you in the prayer vigil. Reflecting on the theme of fatherhood, you will touch the great mystery of God's love. Remember that God is the Father of all of us. It was God who created us, who doles out talents to each of us, who guides us on the path of life, and He is with us, despite our weakness, our sin, our omissions. He wants to save us! He is the model of every family, even the secular. Each of us owes so much to our earthly father, who has given us life, who takes care of us and continues to provide for our daily existence and our growth. Do not forget to give thanks to God for your father! Remember him in prayer even if your relationship should perhaps not be good. Fatherhood is a gift of God and a great responsibility to give a new life, which is an unrepeatable image of God. Do not be afraid of being parents. Many of you will certainly become fathers! Also be open to spiritual fatherhood, a great treasure of our faith. May God give you the richness and radiance of his paternity and fill you with his joy. I cordially greet and bless all pilgrims to the fields of Lednica, the baptismal springs of Poland. I extend this blessing to participants at today's audience, your families and your loved ones. I hope everyone can reap abundant graces from the Solemnity of Corpus Christi.

JESUS, THE BREAD OF GOD FOR HUMANITY

JUNE 2, 2013

ST. PETER'S SQUARE

Dear Brothers and Sisters,

Good morning! Last Thursday we celebrated the Feast of *Corpus Christi*, which, in Italy and in other countries has been moved to this Sunday. It is the Feast of the Eucharist, the sacrament of the Body and Blood of Christ.

The Gospel presents to us the account of the miracle of the Multiplication of the Loaves (Lk 9:11-17); I would like to reflect on one aspect of it that never fails to impress me and makes me think. We are on the shore of the Sea of Galilee, daylight is fading. Jesus is concerned for the people who have spent so many hours with him: there are thousands of them and they are hungry. What should he do? The disciples also pose the problem and tell Jesus:

"Send the crowd away" so that they can go and find provisions in the villages close by. But Jesus says: "You give them something to eat" (v. 13). The disciples are discomfited and answer him: "We have no more than five loaves and two fish," as if to say, barely enough for ourselves.

Jesus well knows what to do, but he wishes to involve his disciples, he wants to teach them. The disciples' attitude is the human one that seeks the most realistic solution which does not create too many problems: dismiss the crowd, they say, let each person organize himself as best he can, moreover you have already done so much for them: you have preached, you have healed the sick . . . *Send the crowd away!*

Looking at those five loaves, Jesus thinks: this is Providence! From this small amount, God can make it suffice for everyone.

Jesus' outlook is very different; it is dictated by his union with the Father and his compassion for the people, that mercifulness of Jesus for us all. Jesus senses our problems, he senses our weaknesses, he senses our needs. Looking at those five loaves, Jesus thinks: this is Providence! From this small amount, God can make it suffice for everyone. Jesus trusts in the heavenly Father without reserve; he knows that for him everything is possible. Thus he tells

19

his disciples to have the people sit down in groups of fifty—this is not merely coincidental, for it means that they are no longer a crowd but become communities nourished by God's bread. Jesus then takes those loaves and fish, looks up to heaven, recites the blessing—the reference to the Eucharist is clear—and breaks them and gives them to the disciples who distribute them . . . and the loaves and fish do not run out, they do not run out! This is the miracle: rather than a multiplication it is a sharing, inspired by faith and prayer. Everyone eats and some is left over: it is the sign of Jesus, the Bread of God for humanity.

The disciples witnessed the message but failed to understand it. Like the crowd they are swept up by enthusiasm for what has occurred. Once again they follow human logic rather than God's, which is that of service, love and faith. The Feast of *Corpus Christi* asks us to convert to faith in Providence, so that we may share the little we are and have, and never to withdraw into ourselves. Let us ask our Mother Mary to help us in this conversion, in order to follow truly and more closely the Jesus whom we adore in the Eucharist. So may it be.

Dear brothers and sisters, my worry about the ongoing war that has been raging in Syria for more than two years is more alive and anguished than ever. It affects in particular the defenseless population that aspires to peace in justice and in understanding. This tormented situation of war brings tragic consequences: death, destruction and immense economic and environmental damage, as well as the scourge of kidnapping people. In deploring these events, I would like to assure those kidnapped and their relatives of my prayers and solidarity, and I appeal to the humanity of the kidnappers to release their victims. Let us continue to pray for our beloved Syria.

There are many situations of conflict in the world but also many signs of hope. I would like to encourage the recent steps toward reconciliation and peace taken by various Latin American countries. Let us accompany them with our prayers.

This morning I celebrated Holy Mass with several soldiers and with the parents of some of those who died in the missions for peace, who seek to further reconciliation and peace in countries in which so much fraternal blood is spilled in wars that are always madness. "Everything is lost in war. Everything is gained with peace." I ask for a prayer for the fallen, for the injured and for their relatives.

Let us now pray together in silence, in our heart—all together—a prayer for the fallen, for the injured and for their relatives. In silence.

I greet with affection all the pilgrims present here today: the families, the faithful of so many parishes, of Italy and of other countries, the associations and movements.

I greet the faithful who have come from Canada and those from Croatia and from Bosnia-Herzegovina, as well as the Piccolo Cottolengo group of Don Orione's Work in Genoa.

I greet everyone. I wish you all a good Sunday and a good lunch!

HUMAN AND ENVIRONMENTAL ECOLOGY GO HAND IN HAND

JUNE 5, 2013

ST. PETER'S SQUARE

Dear Brothers and Sisters, good morning!

Today I would like to reflect on the issue of the environment, as I have already had an opportunity to do on various occasions. I was also prompted to think about this because of today's World Environment Day, sponsored by the United Nations, which is launching a pressing appeal for the need to eliminate waste and the destruction of food.

When we talk about the environment, about creation, my thoughts go to the first pages of the Bible, to the Book of Genesis, where it says that God puts men and women on the earth to till it and keep it (cf. 2:15). And these questions occur to me: What does cultivating and preserving the earth mean? Are we truly cultivating and caring for creation? Or are we exploiting and neglecting it? The verb "cultivate" reminds me of the care a farmer takes to ensure that his land will be productive and that his produce will be shared.

What great attention, enthusiasm and dedication! Cultivating and caring for creation is an instruction of God which he gave not only at the beginning of history, but has also given to each one of us; it is part of his plan; it means making the world increase with responsibility, transforming it so that it may be a garden, an inhabitable place for us all. Moreover on various occasions Benedict XVI has recalled that this task entrusted to us by God the Creator requires us to grasp the pace and the logic of creation. Instead we are often guided by the pride of dominating, possessing, manipulating and exploiting; we do not "preserve" the earth, we do not respect it, we do not consider it as a freely given gift to look after.

We are losing our attitude of wonder, of contemplation, of listening to creation and thus we no longer manage to interpret in it what Benedict XVI calls "the rhythm of the love-story between God and man." Why does this happen? Why do we think and live horizontally? We have drifted away from God, we no longer read his signs.

However "cultivating and caring" do not only entail the relationship between us and the environment, between man and creation. They also concern human relations. The popes have spoken of a *human ecology*, closely connected with *environmental ecology*. We are living in a time of crisis; we see it in the environment, but above all we see it in men and women. The human person is in danger: this much is certain—the human person is in danger today, hence the urgent need for human ecology! And the peril is grave, because the cause of the problem is not superficial but deeply rooted. It is not merely a question of economics but of ethics and anthropology. The Church has frequently stressed this; and many are saying: yes, it is right, it is true . . . but the system continues unchanged since what

> **God the Creator requires us to grasp the pace and the logic of creation.**

dominates are the dynamics of an economy and a finance that are lacking in ethics. It is no longer man who commands, but money, money, cash commands. And God our Father gave us the task of protecting the earth—not for money, but for ourselves: for men and women. We have this task! Nevertheless men and women are sacrificed to the idols of profit and consumption: it is the "culture of waste." If a computer breaks it is a tragedy, but poverty, the needs and dramas of so many people end up being considered normal. If on a winter's night, here on the Via Ottaviano—for example—someone dies, that is not news. If there are children in so many parts of the world who have nothing to eat, that is not news, it seems normal. It cannot be so! And yet these things enter into normality: that some homeless people should freeze to death on the street—this doesn't make news. On the contrary, when the stock market drops ten points in some cities, it constitutes a tragedy. Someone who dies is not news, but lowering income by ten points is a tragedy! In this way people are thrown aside as if they were trash.

This "culture of waste" tends to become a common mentality that infects everyone. Human life, the person, are no longer seen as a primary value to be respected and safeguarded, especially if they are poor or disabled, if they are not yet useful—like the unborn child—or are no longer of any use—like the elderly person. This culture of waste has also made us insensitive to wasting and throwing out excess foodstuffs, which is especially condemnable when, in every part of the world, unfortunately, many people and families suffer hunger and malnutrition. There was a time when our grandparents were very careful not to throw away any leftover food. Consumerism has induced us to be accustomed to excess and to the daily waste of food, whose value, which goes far beyond mere financial parameters, we are no longer able to judge correctly.

Let us remember well, however, that whenever food is thrown out it is as if it were stolen from the table of the poor, from the hungry! I ask everyone to reflect on the problem of the loss and waste of food, to identify ways and approaches which, by seriously dealing with this problem, convey solidarity and sharing with the underprivileged.

A few days ago, on the Feast of Corpus Christi, we read the account of the miracle of the multiplication of the loaves. Jesus fed the multitude with five loaves and two fish. And the end of this passage is important: "And all ate and were satisfied. And they took up what was left over, twelve baskets of broken pieces" (Lk 9:17). Jesus asked the disciples to ensure that nothing was wasted: nothing thrown out! And there is this fact of twelve baskets: why twelve? What does it mean? Twelve is the number of the tribes of Israel, it represents symbolically the whole people. And this tells us that when the food was shared fairly, with solidarity, no one was deprived of what he needed, every

> **Let us remember well that whenever food is thrown out it is as if it were stolen from the table of the poor, from the hungry!**

community could meet the needs of its poorest members. Human and environmental ecology go hand in hand.

I would therefore like us all to make the serious commitment to respect and care for creation, to pay attention to every person, to combat the culture of waste and of throwing out so as to foster a culture of solidarity and encounter. Thank you.

JESUS HAS A HEART OF MERCY

JUNE 9, 2013

ST. PETER'S SQUARE

Dear Brothers and Sisters,

Good morning! The month of June is traditionally dedicated to the Sacred Heart of Jesus, the greatest human expression of divine love. In fact last Friday we celebrated the Solemnity of the Sacred Heart of Jesus and this feast sets the tone for the entire month. Popular piety highly values symbols, and the Heart of Jesus is the ultimate symbol of God's mercy. But it is not an imaginary symbol; it is a real symbol which represents the center, the source from which salvation flowed for all of humanity.

In the Gospels we find various references to the Heart of Jesus. For example there is a passage in which Christ himself says: "Come to me, all who labor and are heavy laden, and I will give you rest. Take my yoke upon you, and learn from me; for I am gentle and lowly in heart" (Mt 11:28-29). Then there is the key account of Christ's death according to John. Indeed this Evangelist bears witness to what he saw on Calvary, that is, when Jesus was already dead a soldier pierced his side with a spear and blood and water came out of the wound (cf. Jn 19:33-34). In that apparently coincidental sign John recognizes the fulfillment of the prophecies: from the Heart of Jesus, the Lamb sacrificed on the Cross, flow forgiveness and life for all people.

The mercy of Jesus is not only an emotion; it is a force which gives life that raises man! Today's Gospel also tells us this in the episode of the widow of Nain (Lk 7:11-17). With his disciples, Jesus arrives in Nain, a village in Galilee, right at the moment when a funeral is taking place. A boy, the only son of a widow, is being carried for burial. Jesus immediately fixes his gaze on the crying mother. The Evangelist Luke says: "And when the Lord saw her, he had compassion on her" (v. 13). This "compassion" is God's love for man, it is mercy, thus the attitude of God in contact with human misery, with our destitution, our suffering, our anguish. The biblical term "compassion" recalls a mother's womb. The mother in fact reacts in a way all her own in confronting the pain of her children. It is in this way, according to Scripture, that God loves us.

What is the fruit of this love and mercy? It is life! Jesus says to the widow of Nain: "Do not weep," and then he calls the dead boy and awakes him as if from sleep (cf. vv. 13-15). Let's think about this, it's beautiful: God's mercy gives life to man, it raises him from the dead. Let us not forget that the Lord always watches over us with mercy; he always watches over us with mercy. Let us not be afraid of approaching him! He has a merciful heart! If we show him our inner wounds, our inner sins, he will always forgive us. It is pure mercy. Let us go to Jesus!

> **Let's think about this, it's beautiful: God's mercy gives life to man, it raises him from the dead.**

Let us turn to the Virgin Mary: her Immaculate Heart, a mother's heart, has fully shared in the "compassion" of God, especially in the hour of the passion and death of Jesus. May Mary help us to be mild, humble and merciful with our brothers.

Today let us not forget the love of God, the love of Jesus: he watches us, he loves us, he waits for us. He is all heart and all mercy. Let us go with faith to Jesus, he always forgives us.

I wish everyone a happy Sunday and have a good lunch!

THE CHURCH, PEOPLE OF GOD

JUNE 12, 2013

ST. PETER'S SQUARE

Dear Brothers and Sisters,

Good morning! Today I would like to reflect on another term by which the Second Vatican Council defined the Church: "People of God" (cf. Dogmatic Constitution *Lumen Gentium*, no. 9; *The Catechism of the Catholic Church*, no. 782). And I do so with several questions for each one of you to reflect on.

1. What does "People of God" mean? First of all it means that God does not belong in a special way to any one people; for it is he who calls us, convokes us, invites us to be part of his people, and this invitation is addressed to all, without distinction, for the mercy of God "desires all men to be saved" (1 Tm 2:4). Jesus does not tell the

Apostles or us to form an exclusive group, a group of the *elite*. Jesus says: go out and make disciples of all people (cf. Mt 28:19). St. Paul says that in the People of God, in the Church, "there is neither Jew nor Greek . . . for you are all one in Christ Jesus" (Gal 3:28). I would also like to say to anyone who feels far away from God and the Church, to anyone who is timid or indifferent, to those who think they can no longer change: the Lord calls you too to become part in his people and he does this with great respect and love! He invites us to be part of this people, the People of God!

2. How does one become a member of this people? It is not through physical birth, but through a new birth. In the Gospel, Jesus tells Nicodemus that he needs to be born from on high, from water and from the Spirit in order to enter the Kingdom of God (cf. Jn 3:3-5). It is through Baptism that we are introduced into this people, through faith in Christ, a gift from God that must be nourished and cultivated throughout our life. Let us ask ourselves: How do I make this faith that I received in my Baptism grow? How do I make this faith that I received and that belongs to the People of God grow?

3. Another question: What is the law of the People of God? It is the law of love, love for God and love for neighbor according to the new commandment that the Lord left to us (cf. Jn 13:34). It is a love, however, that is not sterile sentimentality or something vague, but the acknowledgment of God as the one Lord of life and, at

the same time, the acceptance of the other as my true brother, overcoming division, rivalry, misunderstanding, selfishness; these two things go together. Oh how much more of the journey do we have to make in order to actually live the new law—the law of the Holy Spirit who acts in us, the law of charity, of love! Looking in newspapers or on television we see so many wars between Christians: How does this happen? Within the People of God, there are so many wars! How many wars of envy, of jealousy, are waged in neighborhoods, in the workplace! Even within the family itself, there are so many internal wars! We must ask the Lord to make us correctly understand this law of love.

To pray for those with whom we are angry is a beautiful step toward that law of love.

How beautiful it is to love one another as true brothers and sisters. How beautiful! Let's do something today. We may all have likes and dislikes; many of us are perhaps a little angry with someone; then let us say to the Lord: Lord, I am angry with this or that person; I am praying to you for him or her. To pray for those with whom we are angry is a beautiful step toward that law of love. Shall we take it? Let's take it today!

4. What is this people's mission? It is to bring the hope and salvation of God to the world: to be a sign of the

love of God who calls everyone to friendship with Him; to be the leaven that makes the dough rise, the salt that gives flavor and preserves from corruption, to be a light that enlightens. Look around us—it is enough to open a newspaper, as I said—we see the presence of evil, the Devil is acting. However, I would like to say out loud: God is stronger! Do you believe this, that God is stronger? Let us say it together, let us say it all together: God is stronger! And do you know why he is stronger? Because he is Lord, the only Lord. And I would like to add that reality, at times dark and marked by evil, can change, if we first bring the light of the Gospel especially through our lives. If in a stadium—say the Olympic stadium in Rome or the San Lorenzo in Buenos Aires—on a dark night, if someone turns on a light, you can barely see it but if the other 70,000 spectators turn on their own light, the whole stadium shines. Let our lives together be the one light of Christ; together we will carry the light of the Gospel to the whole of reality.

5. What is the destination of this People? Our destination is the Kingdom of God, which God himself inaugurated on this earth and which must be extended until its fulfillment, when Christ, our life, shall appear (cf. *Lumen Gentium*, no. 9). The end then is full communion with the Lord, familiarity with the Lord, entry into his own divine life, where we will live in the joy of his love beyond measure, a full joy.

Dear brothers and sisters, being the Church, to be the People of God, in accordance with the Father's great design of love, means to be the leaven of God in this humanity of ours. It means to proclaim and to bring God's salvation to this world of ours, so often led astray, in need of answers that give courage, hope and new vigor for the journey. May the Church be a place of God's mercy and hope, where all feel welcomed, loved, forgiven and encouraged to live according to the good life of the Gospel. And to make others feel welcomed, loved, forgiven and encouraged, the Church must be with doors wide open so that all may enter. And we must go out through these doors and proclaim the Gospel.

❧

Today throughout the world the *World Day Against Child Labor* is being celebrated with a special reference to the exploitation of children in domestic work: a deplorable and constantly increasing phenomenon, particularly in poor countries. There are millions of minors, mostly young girls, who are victims of this hidden form of exploitation that often entails abuse as well, mistreatment and discrimination. This really is slavery!

I sincerely hope that the international community can initiate more effective measures to confront this real scourge. All children must be able to play, study, pray and grow, in their own families, and do so in a harmonious context of love and serenity. It is their right and our duty. Many people instead of letting them play make slaves of them: this is a scourge. A serene childhood allows children to look forward with confidence to life and the future. Woe to those who stifle their joyful impulse of hope!

THE GOSPEL OF LIFE

JUNE 16, 2013

ST. PETER'S SQUARE

Dear Brothers and Sisters,

At the end of this Eucharistic Celebration dedicated to the Gospel of Life, I am pleased to recall that yesterday Odardo Focherini, husband and father of seven children, a journalist, was beatified in Carpi. Arrested and incarcerated in hatred of his Catholic faith, he died in the concentration camp of Hersbruck in 1944 at the age of thirty-seven. He saved many Jews from Nazi persecution. Together with the Church in Carpi, let us give thanks to God for this witness to the Gospel of Life!

I warmly thank all of you who have come from Rome and from many parts of Italy and of the world, especially the families and those who are more directly involved in the promotion and protection of life.

I cordially greet the 150 members of the Association "Grávida"-Argentina, gathered in the city of Pilar. Thank you so much for what you have done! Have courage and go forward!

Finally, I greet the many participants in the Harley-Davidson motorcycle rally as well as those from the Motoclub Polizia di Stato [State Police Motoclub].

Let us turn now to Our Lady, entrusting all human life, especially the most fragile, helpless and threatened, to her motherly protection.

THE CHURCH, BODY OF CHRIST

JUNE 19, 2013

ST. PETER'S SQUARE

Dear Brothers and Sisters, good morning!

Today I am pausing to reflect on another expression by which the Second Vatican Council indicates the nature of the Church: body; the Council says that the Church is the Body of Christ (cf. *Lumen Gentium*, no. 7).

I would like to start with a text from the Acts of the Apostles that we know well: the conversion of Saul, later called Paul, one of the greatest evangelizers (cf. Acts 9:4-5). Saul is a persecutor of Christians, but while he is travelling on the road to the city of Damascus, a light suddenly envelops him, he falls to the ground and hears a voice saying to him: "Saul, Saul, why do you persecute me?" He asks: "Who are you, Lord?" and the voice responds: "I am

Jesus whom you are persecuting" (v. 3-5). St. Paul's experience speaks to us of how profound the union between us Christians and Christ really is. When Jesus ascended into heaven he did not leave us orphans, but through the gift of the Holy Spirit our union with him became even more intense. The Second Vatican Council says that "by communicating his Spirit, Christ mystically constitutes as his body those brothers of his who are called together from every nation" (*Lumen Gentium*, no. 7).

The image of the body helps us to understand this profound bond Church-Christ, which St. Paul developed in a particular way in his First Letter to the Corinthians (cf. Chapter 12). First of all, the body reminds us of a living reality. The Church is not a welfare, cultural or political association but a living body that walks and acts in history. And this body has a head, Jesus, who guides, feeds and supports it. This is a point that I would like to emphasize: if one separates the head from the rest of the body, the whole person cannot survive. It is like this in the Church: we must stay ever more deeply connected with Jesus. But not only that: just as it is important that life blood flow through the body in order to live, so must we allow Jesus to work in us, let his Word guide us, his presence in the Eucharist feed us, give us life, his love strengthen our love for our neighbor. And this forever! Forever and ever! Dear brothers and sisters, let us stay united to Jesus, let us trust in him, let us orient our life according to his Gospel, let us be nourished by daily prayer, by listening to the Word of God, by sharing in the Sacraments.

And here I come to a second aspect of the Church as the Body of Christ. St. Paul says that just as the limbs of the human body, although diverse and many, form one body, so have we been baptized by one Spirit into one body (cf. 1 Cor 12:12-13). Consequently, in the Church there is variety and a diversity of roles and functions; there is no flat uniformity, but a wealth of gifts that the Holy Spirit distributes. Yet, there is communion and unity: each one relates to the other and comes together to form a single living body, deeply tied to Christ. Let us remember this well: being part of the Church means being united to Christ and receiving from him the divine life that makes us live as Christians; it means staying united to the Pope and to the Bishops who are instruments of unity and communion; and it also means learning to overcome subjectivism and division, to understand each other better, to harmonize the variety and the richness of each person; in a word to love God and the people beside us more, in the family, in the parish, in associations. Body and limb, in order to live, must be united! Unity is superior to conflict, always! Conflicts, if not properly resolved, divide us from each other, separate us from God. Conflict can help us to grow, but it can also divide us. Let us not go down the path of division, of fighting among ourselves! All united, all united in our differences, but united, always: this is the way of Jesus. Unity is superior to conflict. Unity is a grace for which we must ask the Lord that he may liberate us from the temptation of division, of conflict between us, of selfishness, of gossip. How much evil gossip does, how much evil! Never gossip about others, never! So much damage to the Church comes from division among Christians, from biases, from narrow interests. Division among us, but also division among communities: Evangelical Christians, Orthodox Christians, Catholic Christians, why are we divided? We must

....

Never gossip about others, never! So much damage to the Church comes from division among Christians, from biases, from narrow interests.

try to bring about unity. I will tell you something: today, before leaving home, I spent forty minutes, more or less, half an hour, with an evangelical pastor and we prayed together and sought unity. Because we have to pray together as Catholics and also with other Christians, pray that the Lord give us the gift of unity, unity among us. But how will we have unity among Christians if we are not capable of it among ourselves, as Catholics? Or in our families? So many families fight and are divided! Seek unity, the unity that builds the Church. Unity comes from Jesus Christ. He sends us the Holy Spirit to create unity.

Dear brothers and sisters, let us ask God: help us to be members of the Body of the Church, ever more deeply united to Christ; help us not to cause the Body of the Church to suffer through our conflicts, our divisions, our selfishness. Help us to be living limbs bound one to the other by that unique force, love, which the Holy Spirit pours into our hearts (cf. Rom 5:5).

※

Tomorrow the World Day for Refugees is being celebrated. This year we are asked to consider in particular the situation of refugee families, often forced to flee their homes and homeland suddenly, losing all their possessions and security in order to escape violence, persecution or grave discrimination because of the religion they profess, the ethnic group they belong to or their political ideas.

In addition to the dangers of migration, these families often risk being broken up and, in the countries that receive them, they must come to terms with cultures and societies different from their own. We cannot be insensitive to the families and to all our brothers and sisters who are refugees. We are called to help them, opening ourselves to understanding and hospitality. May people and institutions that help them never be lacking anywhere in the world; their faces reflect the face of Christ!

Last Sunday, during this Year of Faith, on the Day of *Evangelium Vitae*, we celebrated the God who is Life and the source of life, Christ who gives us the gift of divine life, and the Holy Spirit who keeps us in our vital relationship as true children of God. I would like once more to invite everyone to witness to the "Gospel of Life," to promote and defend life in all its dimensions and at every stage. The Christian is the person who says "yes" to life, who says "yes" to God, the Living One . . .

I thank you for coming to this encounter. I ask you to pray for me and for my service to the Church, and I hope that each one of you may receive abundant graces, that you may be reinforced in your generous fidelity to the call of the Lord.

MARTYRDOM, LOSS OF LIFE FOR CHRIST

JUNE 23, 2013

ST. PETER'S SQUARE

Dear Brothers and Sisters, good morning!

In this Sunday's Gospel resound some of Jesus' most incisive words: "Whoever would save his life will lose it; and whoever loses his life for my sake, he will save it" (Lk 9:24).

This is a synthesis of Christ's message, and it is expressed very effectively in a paradox, which shows us his way of speaking, almost lets us hear his voice . . . But what does it mean "to lose one's life for the sake of Jesus"? This can happen in two ways: explicitly by confessing the faith, or implicitly by defending the truth. Martyrs are the greatest example of losing one's life for Christ. In 2,000 years, a vast host of men and women have sacrificed their lives to remain faithful to Jesus Christ and his Gospel. And today, in many parts of the world, there are many, many—more than in the first centuries—so many martyrs, who give up their lives for Christ, who are brought to death because they do not deny Jesus Christ. This is our Church. Today we have more martyrs than in the first centuries! However, there is also daily martyrdom, which may not entail death but is still a "loss of life" for Christ, by doing one's duty with love, according to the logic of Jesus, the logic of gift, of sacrifice. Let us think: how many dads and moms every day put their faith into practice by offering up their own lives in a concrete way for the good of the family! Think about this! How many priests, brothers and sisters carry out their service generously for the Kingdom of God! How many young people renounce their own interests in order to dedicate themselves to children, the disabled, the elderly . . . They are martyrs too! Daily martyrs, martyrs of everyday life!

And then there are many people, Christians and non-Christians alike, who "lose their lives" for truth. And Christ said, "I am the truth," therefore whoever serves the truth serves Christ. One of those who gave his life for the truth is John the Baptist: tomorrow, June 24, is his great feast, the Solemnity of his birth. John was chosen by God to prepare the way for Jesus, and he revealed him to the people of Israel as the Messiah, the Lamb of God who takes away the sin of the world (cf. Jn 1:29). John consecrated himself entirely to God and to his envoy, Jesus. But, in the end, what happened? He died for the sake of the truth, when he denounced the adultery of King Herod and Herodias. How many people pay dearly for their commitment to truth! Upright people who are not afraid to go against the current! How many just men prefer to go against the current, so as not to deny the voice of conscience, the voice of truth! And we, we must not be afraid! Among you are many young people.

> **To you young people I say: Do not be afraid to go against the current!**

To you young people I say: Do not be afraid to go against the current, when they want to rob us of hope, when they propose rotten values, values like food gone bad—and when food has gone bad, it harms us; these values harm us. We must go against the current! And you young people, are the first: Go against the tide and have the daring to move precisely against the current. Forward, be brave and go against the tide! And be proud of doing so.

Dear friends, let us welcome Jesus' words with joy. They are a rule of life proposed to everyone. And may St. John the Baptist help us put that rule into practice. On this path, as always, our Mother, Mary Most Holy, precedes us: she lost her life for Jesus, at the Cross, and received it in fullness, with all the light and the beauty of the Resurrection. May Mary help us to make ever more our own the logic of the Gospel.

Dear brothers and sisters, remember this well: Do not be afraid to go against the current! Be courageous! And like this, just as we do not want to eat food that has gone bad, we will not carry with us rotten values, that ruin life and take away our hope. Forward!

I wish you all a good Sunday! Pray for me and have a good lunch!

GOD BUILT HIS HOUSE AMONG US

JUNE 26, 2013

ST. PETER'S SQUARE

Dear Brothers and Sisters, good morning!

Today I would like to mention briefly another image that helps us describe the mystery of the Church: the temple (cf. Second Vatican Ecumenical Council, Dogmatic Constitution on the Church, *Lumen Gentium*, no. 6).

What does the word "temple" make us think of? It makes us think of a building, of a construction. More especially the minds of many turn to the history of the People of Israel recounted in the Old Testament. Solomon's great Temple in Jerusalem was the place for the encounter with God in prayer. Inside the Temple was the Ark of the Covenant, a sign of God's presence among the people; and the Ark contained the Tables of the Law, the manna and Aaron's rod. This was a reminder that God had always been in the history of his People, that he had accompanied it on its journey and had guided its steps. The Temple is a memorial of this history. When we go to the Temple we too must remember this history, each one of us our own history, how Jesus met me, how Jesus walked beside me, how Jesus loves and blesses me.

It is this that was pre-figured in the ancient Temple and brought about in the Church by the power of the Holy Spirit: the Church is

Let us ask ourselves: Where can we meet God? Where can we enter into communion with him through Christ?

"God's house," the place of his presence, where we can find and encounter the Lord; the Church is the Temple in which the Holy Spirit dwells. It is he who gives life to her, who guides and sustains her. Let us ask ourselves: Where can we meet God? Where can we enter into communion with him through Christ? Where can we find the light of the Holy Spirit to light up our life? The answer is: in the People of God, among us who are the Church. It is here that we shall encounter Jesus, the Holy Spirit and the Father.

The ancient Temple was built by human hands. There was a wish "to give God a house," to have a visible sign of his presence among the people. With the Incarnation of the Son of God, Nathan's prophecy to King David was fulfilled (cf. 2 Sm 7:1-29): it is not the king, it is not we who "give God a house"; rather it is God himself who "builds his house" in order to come and dwell among us, as St. John wrote in his Gospel (cf. 1:14). Christ is the living Temple of the Father, and Christ himself builds his "spiritual house": the Church, not made of material stones but rather of "living stones," which we are. The Apostle Paul said to the Christians of Ephesus: you are "built upon the foundation of the apostles and prophets, Christ Jesus himself being the cornerstone, in whom the whole structure is joined together and grows into a holy temple in the Lord; in whom you also are built . . . for a dwelling place of God in the Spirit" (Eph 2:20-22). This is a beautiful thing! We are the living stones of God's building, profoundly united to Christ who is the keystone and also the one that sustains us. What does this mean? It means that we are the temple, we are the living Church, the living temple, and

> **We are the living stones of God's building, profoundly united to Christ who is the keystone and also the one that sustains us.**

with us when we are together is also the Holy Spirit, who helps us to grow as Church. We are not alone, for we are the People of God: this is the Church!

And it is the Holy Spirit with his gifts who designs the variety. This is important: what does the Holy Spirit do among us? He designs the variety which is a wealth in the Church and unites us, each and every one, to constitute a spiritual temple in which we do not offer material sacrifices but ourselves, our life (cf. 1 Pt 2:4-5). The Church is not a fabric woven of things and interests; she is the Temple of the Holy Spirit, the Temple in which God works, the Temple of the Holy Spirit, the Temple in which God works, the Temple in which, with the gift of Baptism, each one of us is a living stone. This tells us that no one in the Church is useless, and if from time to time someone says to someone else: "Go home, you are no good," this is not true. For no one is no good in the Church, we are all necessary for building this Temple! No one is secondary. No one is the most important person in the Church, we are all equal in God's eyes. Some of you might say "Listen, Mr. Pope, you are not our equal." Yes, I am like each one of you, we are all equal, we are brothers and sisters! No one is anonymous: we all both constitute and build the Church. This also invites us to reflect on the fact that if the brick of our Christian life goes missing, the beauty of the Church loses something. Some people say, "I have nothing to do with the Church"; but in this way the brick of a life in this beautiful Temple is left out.

No one can go away, we must all bring the Church our life, our heart, our love, our thought and our work: all of us together.

I would now like us to ask ourselves: How do we live our being Church? Are we living stones or are we, as it were, stones that are weary, bored or indifferent? Have you ever noticed how grim it is to see a tired, bored and indifferent Christian? A Christian like that is all wrong, the Christian must be alive, rejoicing in being Christian; he or she must live this beauty of belonging to the People of God which is the Church. Do we open ourselves to the action of the Holy Spirit, to be an active part of our communities or do we withdraw into ourselves, saying; "I have so much to do, it isn't my job!"?

The Lord gives all of us his grace, his strength, so that we may be profoundly united to Christ, who is the cornerstone, the pillar and the foundation of our life and of the whole life of the Church. Let us pray that enlivened by his Spirit we may always be living stones of his Church.

PETER AND PAUL, GLORIOUS WITNESSES OF THE LORD

Solemnity of the Holy Apostles

Peter and Paul • June 29, 2013

St. Peter's Square

Dear Brothers and Sisters,

Today, June 29, is the Solemnity of Sts. Peter and Paul, and more especially the Feast of the Church of Rome, founded on the martyrdom of these two Apostles. However, it is also an important feast for the universal Church because the entire People of God is indebted to them for the gift of the faith. Peter was the first to profess that Jesus is the Christ, the Son of God. Paul spread this proclamation throughout the Greek and Roman world.

And Providence ordained that they should both come to Rome and pour out their blood for the faith here. For this reason the Church of Rome immediately, spontaneously, became the reference point for all the Churches scattered across the world. It was not because of the power of the Empire but rather through the mightiness of martyrdom, of the witness borne to Christ! At the core it is always and only the love of Christ that generates faith and carries the Church ahead.

Let us think of Peter. When he professed his faith in Jesus, he did not do so because of his human abilities but rather because he had been won over by the grace that Jesus emanated, by the love he sensed in Jesus' words and saw in his actions: Jesus was God's love personified!

And the same thing happened to Paul, but in a different way. As a young man Paul had been hostile to Christians, and when, on the road to Damascus, the Risen Christ called him, his life was transformed. He understood that Jesus was not dead but living, and even loved him, his former enemy! This is the experience of mercy, of God's forgiveness in Jesus: this is the Good News, the Gospel that Peter and Paul experienced firsthand and for which they laid down their lives. Mercy! Forgiveness! The Lord

> **At the core it is always and only the love of Christ that generates faith and carries the Church ahead.**

always forgives us, the Lord has mercy, he is merciful, he has a merciful heart and always waits for us.

Dear brothers and sisters, what a joy to believe in a God who is all love, all grace! This is the faith that Peter and Paul received from Christ and passed on to the Church. Let us praise the Lord for these two glorious witnesses, and like them let us allow ourselves to be won over by Christ, by the mercy of Christ.

Let us also remember that Simon Peter had a brother, Andrew, who shared with him his experience of faith in Jesus. Indeed, Andrew met Jesus before Simon did, and immediately spoke of him to his brother and took his brother to see Jesus. I am also pleased to remember him because, present in Rome today, in accordance with the beautiful tradition, is the Delegation of the Patriarchate of Constantinople whose Patron is, precisely, the Apostle Andrew. Let us all join in conveying our cordial greeting to Patriarch Bartholomaios I and in praying for him and for this Church. I likewise invite you to pray a *Hail Mary* all together for Patriarch Bartholomaios I; all together: "Hail Mary . . . "

Let us also pray for the Metropolitan Archbishops of various Churches in the world upon whom I have just conferred the Pallium, a symbol of communion and unity.

May our beloved Mother, Mary Most Holy, go with us and sustain us all . . . I wish you all a happy feastday and a good lunch. Goodbye.

THE CONSCIENCE, THE INTERIOR PLACE FOR LISTENING TO GOD

JUNE 30, 2013

ST. PETER'S SQUARE

Dear Brothers and Sisters, good morning!

This Sunday's Gospel Reading (Lk 9:51-62) shows a very important step in Christ's life: the moment when, as St. Luke writes: "He [Jesus] set his face to go to Jerusalem" (9:51). Jerusalem is the final destination where Jesus, at his last Passover, must die and rise again and thus bring his mission of salvation to fulfillment.

From that moment, after that "firm decision" Jesus aimed straight for his goal and in addition said clearly to the people he met and who asked to follow him what the conditions were: to have no permanent dwelling place; to know how to be detached from human affections and not to give in to nostalgia for the past.

Jesus, however, also told his disciples to precede him on the way to Jerusalem and to announce his arrival, but not to impose anything: if the disciples did not find a readiness to welcome him, they should go ahead, they should move on. Jesus never imposes, Jesus is humble, Jesus invites. If you want to, come. The humility of Jesus is like this: he is always inviting but never imposing.

All of this gives us food for thought. It tells us, for example, of the importance which the conscience had for Jesus too: listening in his heart to the Father's voice and following it. Jesus, in his earthly existence, was not, as it were, "remote-controlled": he was the incarnate Word, the Son of God made man, and at a certain point he made the firm decision to go up to Jerusalem for the last time; it was a decision taken in his conscience, but not alone: together with the Father, in full union with him! He decided out of obedience to the Father and in profound and intimate

> **Jesus is humble, Jesus invites. If you want to, come. The humility of Jesus is like this: he is always inviting but never imposing.**

listening to his will. For this reason, moreover, his decision was firm, because it was made together with the Father. In the Father Jesus found the strength and light for his journey. And Jesus was free, he took that decision freely. Jesus wants us to be Christians, freely as he was, with the freedom which comes from this dialogue with the Father, from this dialogue with God. Jesus does not want selfish Christians who follow their own ego, who do not talk to God. Nor does he want weak Christians, Christians who have no will of their own, "remote-controlled" Christians incapable of creativity, who always seek to connect with the will of someone else and are not free. Jesus wants us free. And where is this freedom created? It is created in dialogue with God in the person's own conscience. If a Christian is unable to speak with God, if he cannot hear God in his own conscience, he is not free, he is not free.

This is why we must learn to listen to our conscience more. But be careful! This does not mean following my own ego, doing what interests me, what suits me, what I like . . . It is not this! The conscience is the interior place for listening to the truth, to goodness, for listening to God; it is the inner place of my relationship with him, the One who speaks to my heart and helps me to discern, to understand the way I must take and, once the decision is made, to go forward, to stay faithful.

We have had a marvelous example of what this relationship with God is like, a recent and marvelous example. Pope Benedict XVI gave us this great example when the Lord made him understand, in prayer, what the step was that he had to take. With a great sense of discernment and courage, he followed his conscience, that is, the will of God speaking in his heart. And this example of our Father does such great good to us all, as an example to follow.

Our Lady, in her inmost depths with great simplicity was listening to and meditating on the Word of God and on what was happening to Jesus. She followed her Son with deep conviction and with steadfast hope. May Mary help us to become increasingly men and women of conscience, free in our conscience, because it is in the conscience that dialogue with God takes place; men and women, who can hear God's voice and follow it with determination, who can listen to God's voice, and follow it with decision.

THE CHURCH,
A MISSIONARY
COMMUNITY

JULY 7, 2013

ST. PETER'S SQUARE

Dear Brothers and Sisters! Good morning!

First of all I would like to share with you the joy of having met, yesterday and today, a special pilgrimage for the Year of Faith of seminarians and novices. I ask you to pray for them, that love of Christ may always grow in their lives and that they may become true missionaries of the Kingdom of God.

The Gospel this Sunday (Lk 10:1-12, 17-20) speaks to us about this: the fact that Jesus is not a lone missionary, he does not want to fulfill his mission alone, but involves his disciples. And today we see that in addition to the twelve Apostles he calls another seventy-two, and sends them to the villages, two by two, to proclaim that the Kingdom of God is close at hand. This is very beautiful! Jesus does not want to act alone, he came to bring the love of God into the world and he wants to spread it in the style of communion, in the style of brotherhood. That is why he immediately forms a community of disciples, which is a missionary community. He trains them straight away for the mission, to go forth.

But pay attention: their purpose is not to socialize, to spend time together, no, their purpose is to proclaim the Kingdom of God, and this is urgent! And it is still urgent today! There is no time to be lost in gossip, there is no need to wait for everyone's consensus, what is necessary is to go out and proclaim. To all people you bring the peace of Christ, and if they do not welcome it, you go ahead just the same. To the sick you bring healing, because God wants to heal man of every evil. How many missionaries do this, they sow life, health, comfort to the outskirts of the world. How beautiful it is! Do not live for yourselves, do not live for yourselves, but live to go forth and do good! There are many young people today in the Square: think of this, ask yourselves this: Is Jesus calling me to go forth, to come out of myself to do good? To you, young people, to you boys and girls I ask: you, are you brave enough for this, do you have the courage to hear the voice of Jesus? It is beautiful to be missionaries! . . . Ah, you are good! I like this!

These seventy-two disciples, whom Jesus sent out ahead of him, who were they? Who do they represent? If the Twelve were the Apostles, and also thus represent the Bishops, their successors, these seventy-two could represent the other ordained ministries, priests and deacons; but more broadly we can think of the other ministries in the Church, of catechists, of the lay faithful who engage in parish missions, of those who work with the sick, with different kinds of disadvantaged and marginalized people; but always as missionaries of the Gospel, with the urgency of the Kingdom that is close at hand. Everyone must be a missionary, everyone can hear that call of Jesus and go forth and proclaim the Kingdom!

The Lord's grace is the protagonist! He is the one hero! And our joy is just this: to be his disciples, his friends.

The Gospel says that those seventy-two came back from their mission full of joy, because they had experienced the power of Christ's Name over evil. Jesus says it: to these disciples He gives the power to defeat the evil one. But he adds: "Do not rejoice in this, that the spirits are subject to you; but rejoice that your names are written in heaven" (Lk 10:20). We should not boast as if we were the protagonists: there is only one protagonist, it is the Lord! The

Lord's grace is the protagonist! He is the one hero! And our joy is just this: to be his disciples, his friends. May Our Lady help us to be good agents of the Gospel.

Dear friends, be glad! Do not be afraid of being joyful! Don't be afraid of joy! That joy which the Lord gives us when we allow him to enter our life. Let us allow him to enter our lives and invite us to go out to the margins of life and proclaim the Gospel. Don't be afraid of joy. Have joy and courage!

Dear brothers and sisters,

As you know two days ago the Encyclical Letter on the theme of faith, entitled *Lumen Fidei*, "the light of faith," was promulgated. For the Year of Faith, Pope Benedict XVI began this Encyclical, to follow up those on love and hope. I took up this great work and I brought it to conclusion. I offer it with joy to all the People of God: in fact, especially today, we all need to go to the essence of the Christian Faith, to deepen it and to confront it with our current problems. But I think that this Encyclical, at least in several places, can also be helpful to those in search of God and of the meaning of life. I place it in the hands of Mary, the perfect icon of faith, that she may bring forth the fruit desired by the Lord. . . . To all of you I wish a good Sunday! Have a good lunch! See you soon.

IMITATING THE MERCY OF GOD

JULY 14, 2013

CASTEL GANDOLFO

Dear Brothers and Sisters, good morning,

Today our Sunday meeting for the *Angelus* is taking place here in Castel Gandolfo. I greet the inhabitants of this beautiful little town! Above all, I would like to thank you for your prayers, and I do this with all of you who have come here in large numbers as pilgrims.

Today's Gospel—we are at Chapter 10 of Luke—is the famous Parable of the Good Samaritan. Who was this man? He was an ordinary person coming down from Jerusalem on his way to Jericho on the road that crosses the Judean Desert. A short time before, on that road a man had been attacked by brigands, robbed, beaten and left half dead by the wayside. Before the Samaritan arrived, a priest as well as a Levite had passed by, that is, two people associated with worship in the Lord's Temple. They saw the poor man, but passed him by without stopping. Instead, when the Samaritan saw that man, "he had compassion" (Lk 10:33), the Gospel says. He went to him and bound up his wounds, pouring oil and wine on them; then he set him on his own mount, took him to an inn and paid for his board and lodging . . . in short, he took care of him: this is the example of love of neighbor. However, why does Jesus choose a Samaritan to play the lead in the parable? Because Samaritans were despised by Jews on account of their different religious traditions; and yet Jesus shows that the heart of that Samaritan was good and generous and that—unlike the priest and the Levite—he puts into practice the will of God who wants mercy rather than sacrifices (cf. Mk 12:33). God always wants mercy and does not condemn it in anyone. He wants heartfelt mercy because he is merciful and can understand well our misery, our difficulties and also our sins. He gives all of us this merciful heart of his! The Samaritan does precisely this: he really imitates the mercy of God, mercy for those in need.

A man who lived to the full this Gospel of the Good Samaritan is the Saint we are commemorating today: St. Camillus de Lellis, Founder of the Clerks Regular Ministers to the Sick, Patron of ill people and health-care workers. St. Camillus died on July 14, 1614: this very day his fourth centenary is being inaugurated and will end in a year. I greet with deep affection all the spiritual sons and daughters of St. Camillus who live by his charism of charity in daily contact with the sick. Be "Good Samaritans" as he was! And I hope that doctors, nurses and all those who work in hospitals and clinics may also be inspired by the same spirit. Let us entrust this intention to the intercession of Mary Most Holy.

Moreover I would like to entrust another intention to Our Lady, together with you all. The World Youth Day in Rio de Janeiro is now at hand. One can see that there are many young people here, but you are all young at heart! I shall leave in a week, but many young people will set out for Brazil even sooner. Let us therefore pray for this great pilgrimage which is beginning, that Our Lady of Aparecida, Patroness of Brazil, may guide the footsteps of the participants and open their hearts to accepting the mission that Christ will give them.

Dear brothers and sisters, I join in prayer the Prelates and faithful of the Church in Ukraine, gathered in the Cathedral of Lutsk for a Holy Mass of suffrage on the 70th anniversary of the Volhynia massacres. These acts, incited by the nationalist ideology in the tragic context of the Second World War, took a toll of tens of thousands of victims and wounded the brotherhood of two peoples, the Polish and the Ukrainian. I entrust the victims' souls to God's mercy and for their peoples I ask the grace of profound reconciliation and a serene future in hope and in sincere collaboration for the common edification of the Kingdom of God.

I am also thinking of the Pastors and faithful who are taking part in the pilgrimage of the Family of Radio Maria to Jasna Góra, Częstochowa. I entrust you to the protection of the Mother of God and impart to you a heartfelt blessing . . . I wish you all a good Sunday and a good lunch!

CONTEMPLATION AND SERVICE

July 21, 2013

St. Peter's Square

Dear Brothers and Sisters, good morning!

This Sunday we continue reading the ten chapters of the Evangelist Luke. The passage today is that on Martha and Mary. Who are these two women? Martha and Mary, sisters of Lazarus, are the relatives and faithful disciples of the Lord, who lived in Bethany. St. Luke describes them in this way: Mary, at the feet of Jesus, "listened to his teaching," while Martha was burdened with much serving (cf. Lk 10:39-40). Both welcome the Lord on his brief visit, but they do so differently. Mary sets herself at the feet of Jesus to listen but Martha lets herself become absorbed in preparing everything, and so much so that she says to Jesus: "Lord, do you not care that my sister has left me to serve alone? Tell her then to help me" (v. 40). And Jesus answers scolding her sweetly: "Martha, Martha, you are anxious and worried about many things. There is need of only one thing" (v. 41).

What does Jesus mean? What is this one thing that we need? First of all, it is important to understand that this is not about two contradictory attitudes: listening to the word of the Lord, contemplation, and practical service to our neighbor. These are not two attitudes opposed to one another, but, on the contrary, they are two essential aspects in our Christian life; aspects that can never be separated, but are lived out in profound unity and harmony. Why then was Martha scolded, even if kindly, by Jesus? Because she considered only what she was doing to be essential; she was too absorbed and worried by the things "to do." For a Christian, works of service and charity are never detached from the principle of all our action: that is, listening to the Word of the Lord, to be—like Mary—at the feet of Jesus, with the attitude of a disciple. And that is why Martha was scolded.

In our Christian life too, dear brothers and sisters, may prayer and action always be deeply united. A prayer that does not lead you to practical action for your brother—the poor, the sick, those in need of help, a brother in difficulty—is a sterile and incomplete prayer. But, in the same way, when ecclesial service is attentive only to doing, things gain in importance, functions, structures, and we forget the centrality of Christ. When time is not

71

set aside for dialogue with him in prayer, we risk serving ourselves and not God present in our needy brother and sister. St. Benedict sums up the kind of life that indicated for his monks in two words: *ora et labora*, pray and work. It is from contemplation, from a strong friendship with the Lord that the capacity is born in us to live and to bring the love of God, his mercy, his tenderness, to others. And also our work with brothers in need, our charitable works of mercy, lead us to the Lord, because it is in the needy brother and sister that we see the Lord himself.

> **A prayer that does not lead you to practical action for the poor, the sick, those in need of help, a brother in difficulty, is a sterile and incomplete prayer.**

Let us ask the Virgin Mary, the Mother of listening and of service, to teach us to meditate in our hearts on the Word of her Son, to pray faithfully, to be ever more attentive in practical ways to the needs of our brothers and sisters.

❧

I see written down there: "Buon viaggio!" [Have a good trip]. Thank you! Thank you! I ask that you accompany me in spirit with your prayers throughout my first Apostolic Journey which I will begin tomorrow. As you know, I will travel to Rio de Janeiro in Brazil for the 28th World Youth Day. There will be many young people there, from every part of the world. And I think that this could be called the Week for Youth: that's it, the Week for Youth! The heroes of this week will be the youth. All those who come to Rio wanting to hear the voice of Jesus, to listen to Jesus: "Lord, what should I do with my life? What is the path for me?" You too—I don't know whether there are young people here in the square today! Are there young people? There they are: you too, young people in the square, ask that same question of the Lord: "Lord Jesus, what should I do with my life? What is the path for me?" Let us entrust to the intercession of the Blessed Virgin Mary, so loved and venerated in Brazil, this question: what the young people there will do, and what you will do, today. And may Our Lady help us in this new stage of the pilgrimage.

To all of you I wish a good Sunday! Enjoy your lunch. Farewell!